For the Love of Lentil

FOR
THE
L(OF)VE
LENTIL

A journey of longing, loss and abundant grace

Sarah Moore

Matador
9 Priory Business Park,
Wistow Road, Kibworth Beauchamp,
Leicestershire. LE8 0RX
Tel: 0116 279 2299
Email: books@troubador.co.uk
Web: www.troubador.co.uk/matador
Twitter: @matadorbooks

ISBN 978 178901 540 9

British Library Cataloguing in Publication Data.
A catalogue record for this book is available from the British Library.

Printed on FSC accredited paper
Printed and bound in Great Britain by 4edge Limited

Typeset in 11pt Minion Pro by Troubador Publishing Ltd, Leicester, UK

Back cover image by Tom Kay

Matador is an imprint of Troubador Publishing Ltd

Contents

Acknowledgements

This book, and the journey it follows, would not have been possible without the love and support of my husband Gary, our family, church family and wider circle of friends. Particular thanks must go to Mike and Fiona, for the support they have been through so much of this journey, and to Ian and De who, between them and without realising it, gave me the confirmation I needed that I should make this book a reality and the impetus to do it.

But first and foremost this book is written in honour of our precious Lentil, who was at the centre of this journey, and of God, who now holds our darling child safely in his ever-loving arms.

Introduction

There are times in life that leave us questioning our understanding. Whether a little or a lot, we find ourselves rethinking things we thought we understood – previously-certain concepts around which we'd shaped parts of our existence. There are times when we think we understand where things are going and how life is panning out, only to have the rug pulled out from under us and find ourselves staring up at the ceiling wondering how we came to be so far off what we thought was a certain course.

One such time, for me, was my husband and I losing our first baby to miscarriage. After a long and challenging path to become pregnant, we felt utterly certain God had answered our deepest prayers when we found out we were expecting a child. We were overwhelmed with love, excitement and gratitude and eagerly began to prepare for what we thought lay ahead.

Nothing could have prepared us for the devastation we would face just weeks later when we learned that our tiny but utterly-precious child had died. We faced immense grief and, alongside it, confusion over our understanding of God's plan for our lives.

Amid all the work of facing up to our loss, our return to childlessness and the almost-overwhelming heartache that accompanied them, one thing quickly became crystal clear; if God's plan wasn't to bring our baby to birth and place him in our arms, He must have had a greater plan to bless people through our circumstances. Our task was simply to discover our part in that plan.

And that is how this book came about. As we began to share our news, we saw people being impacted in ways we never imagined, through our words, by the power of God's love and grace in our lives. We have no idea who God plans to bless through this book or how; we're simply being faithful to the call we believe He has put on us to share our story of His love, grace and faithfulness.

You might be reading this having been through experiences similar to ours or the path of your life might have been entirely different. Either way, it doesn't matter. No two people's experiences will ever be exactly the same (even Gary and I experienced our miscarriage differently) but one common theme runs through every journey – that God can wrap His loving arms around each one of us and lead us on through the darkest times into the light of His love.

The following pages bring together reflections on our journey, journal notes from along the way and songs placed in my heart by God at key times that had an impact as we travelled through some of our darkest days.

God has taught me so much through this journey and I hope that in some small way He will use it to teach others something too.

ONE

The beginning of the journey

From the day we married in spring 2013, Gary and I always anticipated that we'd go on to be parents. We loved children, we enjoyed spending time with our nieces as they grew up, we were often the first to play silly games with friends' little ones. We'd spent the months prior to our wedding going through the process of becoming foster carers, offering weekend respite placements that would fit around our full-time jobs. We'd anticipated that in the future we might be in a position to extend what we offered to children in foster care if our family circumstances changed and one or both of us ended up working fewer hours. We'd never questioned that one day we would have a child of our own.

We'd always planned to spend at least the first year of married life just as two, and even after that we didn't rush hell for leather into trying to become parents. Who wants to feel like a would-be tiny-human factory? But after two or three years we moved from a take-no-precautions-and-if-it-happens-it-happens approach to actively seeking to conceive.

We weren't naïve about the fertility difficulties couples can experience but we had no reason to suspect that, for us, becoming pregnant would be anything other than a simple and relatively-quick process. We were young, healthy, relatively fit (okay, there was room for improvement on my part). There was nothing to ring alarm bells in our minds.

We hoped and prayed for a baby and longed for an answer to our prayers. In June 2015 I attended a Christian women's conference and when the opportunity arose to pray I prayed hard that God would grant us the baby we so desired. I was filled with the buzz of the event and with the refreshing that comes with taking time out to focus on God. I felt certain He would grant our wish, and soon. I'd asked for it at a really big event and the music was really loud and stuff so obviously God was going to answer that prayer, 'cause that's how it works, right? (Yes, I'd watched the comedy film Bruce Almighty. I knew God couldn't and wouldn't just say "yes" to every prayer. Still I couldn't see a reason why He wouldn't answer mine.) Answers to prayer were all around. We knew the work He had done in so many lives. He loved us like He loved them so surely it would be our turn soon – surely. Surely?

I sensed that God wanted us to share our prayer with others and bring them in to stand alongside us in that prayer. I suppressed that sense. That was probably partly because I didn't want to seem like I was being greedy asking for stuff for me, even though I knew God was a loving Father who longed to lavish blessing on His children. It was probably partly because I was totally abysmal at letting people in however much I tried to convince myself I didn't put up barriers (I imagine I was probably better at fooling myself there than I was anyone else but they were gracious and they didn't say as much). And, if I was totally honest, it was partly because I was scared God wouldn't answer – or at least wouldn't give me the answer I wanted – and it's one thing to be disappointed but another for other people to know it.

As time progressed we realised things weren't going to be as simple as we'd hoped. We'd begin each month in eager expectation that this could be the month. We'd end each month in disappointment which, as time wore on, lurched towards despair and disbelief.

Twelve months came and went after the conference – 12 long months – another 12 months of disappointment. We seemed no closer to realising our dream. Maybe it was just a dream. Maybe God's way of saying "no" to us was to say nothing and wait for us to take the hint. Maybe we were being selfish wanting something more in life when we had already been blessed with so much. Maybe we were overthinking. Maybe we weren't thinking enough. Maybe we just wanted to know one way or another.

TWO

Being obedient

A year later I found myself back at the same women's conference. There, again, came an opportunity for 7,000 women to each pray for the miracle they wanted God to do in their lives. I offered up my prayer but my mind was so different to the previous year. Then I had been so full of expectation that God would not only hear but answer my prayer, and answer it in the way I wanted. Maybe I was bolstered by the sheer size of the event, the power of the music, the bright lights. Maybe not. Who knows? A year on I had lived through 12 months of disappointment and the growing sense that God was hearing my prayers and choosing not to answer them, and I didn't know why. But still I asked and still I knew God could grant us the overwhelming desire of our hearts if He wanted to, and I had to hope and believe that He wanted to.

As I prayed I felt a real sense that God was responding. His message seemed clear; if we wanted an answer to our prayer we needed to bring in other people to join us in that prayer. That would never be an easy thing to do. We'd never been the types to wear our hearts on our sleeves and sharing with others about something so deeply personal was not an idea we relished. It's one thing knowing as a couple the disappointment you face every month that you realise you're still not expecting, but quite another to know that someone else can see it in you. Plus there was always the risk that we'd never fulfil our dream of becoming parents and other people would know about our unfulfilled longing. Neither filled us with great enthusiasm for shouting our prayer from the rooftops at anyone who'd listen.

The night I returned from the conference was the night of our monthly prayer gathering at church. I turned up. It seemed silly not to in the circumstances. Maybe this was the day I would call on people to join us in praying for our miracle. Somebody asked me if there wasn't anything I wanted prayer for. I couldn't have been given a better opportunity. I said there wasn't. Maybe I was overcome with fear about opening up. Maybe my subconscious felt I'd not had sufficient time to discuss with Gary the possibility of sharing something so personal to us with a wider audience (not that I would have shared the details at that stage; I'd simply have asked them to join us in praying for the miracle and left the details between me, Gary and God). Somebody else said something that gave me another perfect opportunity. Whatever the reason – and it was probably fear – I bottled it, again, and I could have kicked myself for doing it.

At the end of the meeting a good friend asked if I was okay and I said I was fine. I knew I wasn't. He knew I wasn't. It was all I could do not to burst into tears, but I had barriers and signs of weakness to think about. In my mind I couldn't possibly have let anyone think I didn't have it all together, because somehow I was actually naïve enough to think I was fooling people when I was probably fooling myself more than anyone else. Everyone else left and I stayed behind and sent that friend an email and, to avoid completely failing to do what God couldn't have made clearer He wanted me to do if He'd sent a massive neon sign with it written on and then set fire to it, I asked him to join us in praying for our miracle.

I knew that no circumstance was too small for God to care about and that no circumstance of someone else's life was so big that it would prevent Him wanting to act in mine too. And now I had a renewed hope that He would act in mine.

In the days that followed we came to share the details of our prayer with this friend and he and his wife became our prayer partners. Finally, we were in the place God had said we should put ourselves in 12 months earlier. I was slow on the uptake – or at least in the obedience – but I'd got there in the end.

THREE

My not-even-Christmas list

Summer 2016 was a time of uncertainty for me. I had longed for a child for so long. I felt God had been speaking to me about things I needed to do to bring to fruition my desire to be a mother. Yet I began to question whether parenthood was really in God's plan for my life. Doubts crept into my mind, complete with fears not only that I might never have a child but that, in my striving for that which I was not to have, I might miss the even greater blessing that God had lined up for me. We so wanted a child of our own and we knew God could make it happen, but at the same time we called on Him to help us not to doubt His plans for us if they did not feature a child.

Over time God worked in our lives in lots of little ways putting in building blocks towards the bigger heart change that was needed in me. He blessed us with more ways to make a difference in children's lives and showed me that I didn't need to be a parent to have a positive impact on His children.

I felt God speak into my heart to remind me that there were things so much more precious to seek after, like being constantly filled with the Holy Spirit to outwork His plans. I called on God to refocus my mind and my longings and keep my eyes fixed on Him as the ultimate gift.

Then at a prayer meeting on September 4 I was reminded that God wants to lavish blessings upon His children and that He calls on us to ask Him for things. Luke chapter 11, verses 11-13, says, "Which of you fathers, if your son asks for a fish, will give him a snake instead? Or if he asks for an egg, will give him a scorpion? If you then, though you are evil, know how to give good gifts to your children, how much more will your Father in heaven give the Holy Spirit to those who ask him!" In the same way that a child writes a Christmas list to guide his parents in what to buy him, we set about writing our not-even-Christmas lists (after all, September is a bit early to write an actual Christmas list if you're no longer five). And at the top of mine I placed the words, "I pray for a baby of our own."

Again I was filled with hope. God had given me a fresh and different opportunity to pray for the child we so wanted. He had reminded me that the Father wants to lavish His children with abundant blessings far greater than those of an earthly father. He'd reminded me He wanted us to ask Him for those blessings. Why would He lead me to write this list if He didn't intend to grant me the gifts I had listed?

I copied my list into my journal when I got home and revisited it regularly in my prayer time. I put my trust fully in God and the belief that He wanted me to soon cross some of my requests off that list as granted.

FOUR

God sees me where I am

A week later, on September 11, 2016, God shook my perspective on my longing and waiting. In a moment of humbling realisation He brought me back to the cross and reminded me of the ultimate promises and truth in my life: that God loved me so much that Jesus died to save me and give me eternal life and glory. I quickly realised I had been allowing my frustration at my childlessness and the perceived lack of answer to our prayers to become a barrier to a full relationship with God. I had allowed questions like "But, if God loves me, why…?" and "He can do all things so why not this?" to creep into my mind.

With a gentleness that only God can display, He brought me back to the massive, all-consuming central reality of our relationship: John 3:16, that "…God so loved the world that he gave his one and only Son, that whoever believes in him shall not perish but have eternal life." This was the greatest gift I could ever receive. I had allowed myself to be so consumed by the desire to be a mother that I had begun to see a baby as the only gift that mattered but this was so, so much more. I'd sung songs about Jesus dying for my sins but I'd allowed myself to become blasé about the reality behind them. I had seemed to gloss over what God had given me as easily as one might mention in passing that somebody had given them a box of chocolates or a bunch of flowers.

The reality that God brought home to me in that moment, sitting in a time of quiet contemplation in my favourite lakeside walking spot, was massive. Jesus died a slow and agonising death despite never doing anything wrong so that I could be forgiven for all the wrong things I do. "For God did not send his Son into the world to condemn the world, but to save the world through him." (John 3:17)

And what struck me more plainly than it had ever struck me before was that Jesus didn't die simply to pay the price for the wrongdoing I would do before I came to know Him; He died that slow, agonising death also as the ransom for all the mistakes I would continue to make after He first cleansed me of my sins, even those I'd made in my walk with Him by putting my desire for a child ahead of my desire to be fully in step with Him.

I had had the audacity to think "if God would only do this one thing for me" when He had already done so, so much that I did not and do not deserve. He had saved me from an eternity in hell. He had my back and I knew He only wanted the best for me. What I had presumed to know better than He did was what that "best" was.

I knew that I truly owed my life to Jesus and in that moment I offered it up to Him afresh and called on Him to be sovereign of it and do with it as He wished. If that plan included me being a mum I would relish the role, but I called on Him to help me, if it didn't, to accept that it had to be His will, not mine, Gary's or anyone else's, that reigned supreme in our lives.

In that moment I called upon God to guard me against measuring my achievements based on the world's model of success and to remind me that success to God means something very different. I called on God to have total charge of my life.

And at the bottom of the journal pages on which I had poured our my heart I found these two verses:

"You have made known to me the path of life; you will fill me with joy in your presence, with eternal pleasures at your right hand." Psalm 16:11

"As for God, his way is perfect: the Lord's word is flawless; he shields all who take refuge in him." 2 Samuel 22:31

And on that day God put on my heart the words of Romans 12:12, which have stayed with me and spoken so much to me with every step of my walk since then: "Be joyful in hope, patient in affliction, faithful in prayer."

On that day, I wrote the following entry in my journal, which summed up where I saw myself in God's creation:

As the blade of grass sways in the field,
God sees it.
As the wave laps at the shore,
God hears it.
As the wind rushes through the trees,
God feels it.
Every grain of sand, He has counted.
Every hair on your head, He knows.
When a sparrow falls from the sky, He notices its passing.

Everything created came from Him.
Everything in nature that moves does so at His command.
The sun does not rise but for Him giving the instruction.

And yet – and yet – He has time for me.
In a world of seven billion people, He has time for me.
He wants to spend time with me as I seek to spend time with Him.
He wants to spend time with me even when I let life's trivialities distract
me from spending time with Him.
He sees my sleeping and my waking.
He sees my toil and my rest.

He knows the words on my lips even before they have formed on the
thoughts of my mind, even before they have filtered into my brain.

He knows the desires of my heart today but, greater than that, He knows
the desires that will be on my heart tomorrow.
Some He will grant. Some He won't. Each decision, I know, He takes
for my best interests.

His plan for my life is immeasurably better than any plan I could draw up for myself.
I can only wonder at where the next path will take me on my journey with Him, ever knowing He is at my side in companionship, before me leading the way and behind me urging me on.

I am in awe at His greatness, His generosity and His love, yet I can understand so little of it with my human mind.

One day all will be revealed.
Until then I will continue to walk by faith into the great things He has set out for me and not by sight into the limited things I can see for myself.

FIVE

A time of uncertainty

Following the construction of my not-even-Christmas list, it would be easy to think the challenges I faced would be over. God wants to lavish His children with blessings, I'd asked Him to bless us with a baby so He was bound to do that and all I needed to do was wait patiently and faithfully, and probably not for much longer. The difficulty with that illustration, of course, is that we don't live in a fairy tale. We live in the real world and, in the real world, we don't see every prayer answered in the way we would like – and they can't be because sometimes the outworking of one person's prayer directly contradicts what another is seeking (you only need to watch Bruce Almighty to understand that, not that I'm advocating that as a leading source of biblical truth).

We're not set apart by God to live a name-it-and-claim-it Christian life in which He grants us everything we would quite like to have (which might explain why I don't live in a big country house with a swimming pool, staff, several posh cars and a couple of ponies).

We are set apart to live a Christian life in which God gives us everything we need, and sometimes that which we need looks very different to that which we want.

And, for that reason, we faced further uncertainty on our path to answered prayer. It probably wasn't helped by my startling ability to overthink or my insatiable desire to be able to have advanced revelation of the outcome of every situation I find myself in. I hated not knowing whether our prayer would ever be answered and I hated the fact that, because I didn't know that, I didn't know whether I was even doing the right thing by praying.

So, for many months, I followed a path that lurched from one extreme to the other, either praying earnestly for a baby and believing God would absolutely grant us one and it would almost undoubtedly be "this month" or resolving that it might not be God's will for us to have a child, we should probably give up focusing on it in case it wasn't, so that we didn't waste our lives seeking something unachievable, and we should leave it for God to grant us a baby if He chose to, but not actively pursue it.

One of the difficulties I faced in trying to correctly attune my focus to bring it in line with where God wanted me was the fact that there were clear merits in both poles. Mark 11:24 tells us: "Therefore I tell you, whatever you ask for in prayer, believe that you have received it, and it will be yours." John 15:7 says: "If you remain in me and my words remain in you, ask whatever you wish, and it will be done for you." Yet Proverbs 19:21 tells us: "Many are the plans in a person's heart, but it is the Lord's purpose that prevails." And 1 Thessalonians 5:16-18 says: "Rejoice always, pray continually, give thanks in all circumstances; for this is God's will for you in Christ Jesus."

While it is easy to find supposed contradiction between the assertion that God will grant heartfelt prayers and the assertion that God's will is greater than our will, the fact that both appear in the Bible is a clear indication that they must, one way or another, work in harmony. That is to say, while they appear at face value to be mutually exclusive, it's clear that they're not. The challenge is simply to understand, from the limited perspective of human logic and reason, how that can be. One conclusion that can be reached is that those who are truly in the Lord, are fully absorbed in His Word and are genuinely walking His path will have their hearts so attuned to God's heart that they will begin to think as He thinks, desire what He desires and pray for that which is His will.

And, from there, the logical conclusion one can draw, when the desired answer to prayer is not forthcoming, is that there is something amiss in one's walk with God. Maybe I didn't believe like I thought I believed. Maybe I didn't really have the faith I needed that God could and would answer my prayer. Maybe I didn't spend enough time with God, or I misunderstood His Word or the leadings I thought He was giving me, or maybe I was kidding myself to think He would really want to bless me. I felt I needed to better understand God's will for my life but as He didn't seem to be demonstrating it to me I didn't know how I could achieve that. Ultimately, I wanted a sign from Him about whether it was His plan for us to be parents, so we would know whether to bother pursuing it or not. It's clear to see, in retrospect, the fallibility of that desire. If God made it clear to us that He wanted us to be parents – or not to be parents – there would be no need for us to have faith, and if we didn't need faith we would be all the poorer for it. But, at that time, I wanted clarity and certainty.

Then, on November 2, 2016, I felt I'd got it. We'd previously come to the point of deciding we should stop seeking to be parents and leave things in God's hands to bless us with a baby if He chose to and to put us on an alternative path if He didn't. God had reminded me in early October that we were made complete in Him and we needed nothing apart from Him to make us complete. Therefore, to have a baby would be nice but we didn't need to be parents, or anything else, to make us whole. But on November 2, we were challenged, by discussion during a course we were working through at church, to not just pray for things but to have real faith for those prayers to be answered. And at that time I felt a clear leading from God that we should be filled with faith that He would answer our prayer and demonstrate that by buying an outfit to dress our little baby in when he blessed us with one.

I questioned whether it was really God putting this on my heart or if it was my own mind, but I knew I would never have put it on my own heart to step out in this way because of the risk of disappointment that could follow. It must have been from God. I thought about waiting until we were expecting a baby to buy something but then I realised that shopping for baby clothes when you're pregnant is an act of necessity, not an act of faith, and it was an act of faith that God wanted from us. I thought of Noah and the fact that building an ark before the flood came looked bizarre and foolish but God had told him to do it, God knew why and Noah knew he needed to be obedient to God.

Filled with a sense of relief that God hadn't asked me to build a massive boat, I left the church building after the session and went straight to buy a little outfit and blanket, discussing it with Gary on the way. Like so many women, I don't need much encouragement to shop for clothes, particularly those as cute as baby clothes, so I was happy to obey. I bought a sweet little outfit and, in the weeks that followed, we periodically brought it out of its storage place as we prayed for God to grant us the child we so desired and commanded whatever barriers were preventing that happening to be broken down. We had a renewed hope and a renewed contentment, not just content to receive whatever God chose to give us but content in our belief that God wanted to give us the answer to prayer we so longed for.

SIX

Seeking joy, patience and faithfulness

Throughout our journey towards becoming parents, one Bible verse remained at the centre of my thoughts and prayers on the topic. Romans 12:12 reminded me of the need to, "Be joyful in hope, patient in affliction, faithful in prayer." Some bits came more easily than others. Faithful prayer became second nature. I knew God could give me the answer I so wanted and, when I was set on wanting it, I was relentless in asking for it. But it's fair to say joy and patience in the matter became somewhat more sporadic. It was relatively easy to be joyful in the days filled with the hope that this could be the month. It came far less easily on the days after we realised it wouldn't be. And, as my mind wandered and thought of just how many of those months there had been, and the fact that they were ever growing in number, patience did not often come easily.

But, on many occasions, as I wrestled with disappointment,

sadness and unfulfilled longing, coupled with fears that maybe I wasn't doing all I could to realise our dream, and doubts that we would ever get there, God gently brought me back to Romans 12:12 and reminded me of the need to be patient. And, time after time, I prayed that I would be patient and not lose hope, faith or trust.

Looking back perhaps praying for patience wasn't the wisest move in the circumstances. After all, how can you be taught patience without being made to wait for something? Maybe I shot myself in the foot there in terms of that for which we were ultimately hoping, but never was it a shot in the foot when it came to my overall walk with God.

Amid the turmoil there were months when my joy, patience and faith weren't shaken despite the realisation that another four weeks had passed without our prayers being answered. On those occasions, joy didn't give way to despair, patience was not replaced with deep sadness and faithfulness wasn't overcome by painful longing. And when that happened I knew God was at work in me, and, at times, I saw that the fact He had not yet answered my prayers enabled me to serve Him in ways I couldn't have done had I been pregnant. He had the bigger picture and His was the perfect plan. I knew that being part of the outworking of God's plan in whatever way he lined up for me was far more fulfilling than anything I could ever dream or plan for myself, and greater even than motherhood on my terms could be.

I found that I was content, but not in the sense that I was satisfied with not actively seeking parenthood. I had thought I was content with that previously and realised how wrong I had been. Now I redefined what contentment meant in my life – to be content with the here and now God had provided for me while praying ceaselessly for a child. Operation Contentedness was born and, when challenges hit, I ploughed my efforts into remembering to embrace the here and now, as well as seeking that which we wanted for the future.

As 2017 dawned, I reflected on what could be to come in the months ahead. "As we enter this new year, Lord, I feel a definite sense that this is going to be the best yet for me and Gary," I wrote in my journal. "I feel a sure and certain hope that this year You will bless us with the baby we so desire."

SEVEN

Counting our blessings

As time went on I focused on trying to keep myself in check and maintain perspective. I say "trying" because I know I didn't always achieve it but, as far as I could, I reminded myself of the many blessings in my life. Though it was impossible not to be very aware of the one thing we so keenly wanted but still didn't have, I set out to focus on all the good gifts God had lavished – and continued to lavish – on us. When I found myself creeping into the oh-so-easy mindset of "If God loves me, why doesn't He…?" I tried to focus on all the things He had given us. We had good health. So many people did not. We had jobs and a comfortable income. So many people did not. We had a roof over our heads, money to heat our home, clean clothes on our backs, food in our stomachs and more besides. So many people were so much worse off than us. And we were blessed with a host of supportive family and friends. We lacked no good thing.

What was more, I knew we didn't need any of those things – at least not in the abundance with which we had them – to prove to us that God loved us. We knew He loved us. We knew, as Philippians 4:19 tells us, that He would provide for all our needs. And, ultimately, we knew He had provided for our ultimate need of salvation by sending Jesus to take the punishment for all our sins (even those we still committed by falling into the trap of doubt). God didn't need to prove that He loved us. Not being parents didn't make us any less loved or lovable (and, let's face it, it was thanks to God's great grace that He loved us, because we weren't very loveable until we were washed clean by Him).

Time after time God reminded me that I needed nothing apart from Him, that I was made complete in Him and that I needed nothing else in my life to make me whole. From time to time I lost focus, but ultimately I knew I rested safe and secure on that knowledge. He was our all in all. If He granted us a child, all to the good. If He didn't, we would be no less complete. And, if He didn't, it would mean other opportunities to serve God's purposes and be part of His perfect plan. Whatever the plan, the prospect of being any part of it was an exciting one.

Isaiah 54:1 instructs: "Sing, barren woman, you who never bore a child; burst into song, shout for joy, you who were never in labour; because more are the children of the desolate woman than of her who has a husband,' says the Lord." And I knew I had a responsibility to sing joyfully to the Lord, whatever my circumstances, because ultimately He had paid the ransom for my life and promised me an inheritance greater than any I could ever earn, not because of who I was, but because of who He was, is and always will be. I felt certain He had promised to lavish us with the further blessing of a child – all I needed to do was not worry about the "when".

EIGHT

My strength and my fortress

Psalm 18 is a declaration of God's all-encompassing, fully-sustaining part in the lives of His people. It begins, in verses 1-2: "I love you, Lord, my strength. The Lord is my rock, my fortress and my deliverer; my God is my rock, in whom I take refuge, my shield and the horn of my salvation, my stronghold." It is so true. As I continued to pray for a child, I knew that all that I was was in God and all that I had was from God. He may not have answered this one prayer, yet, but He blessed me abundantly even in ways I did not see, protecting me from dangers I did not even realise I faced. He was there in the good times and He was there to draw me close and comfort me whenever I was distressed. He was my all in all. He was never to blame for my distress but was always there as the first to call on in my distress. And His plans for me were perfect and intended only to prosper me, not to harm me. He was the one good thing in which all my life, my hope and my being were grounded and I clung to Him with every step and stood confident in Him with every breath.

I knew that God deserved my praises. I owed Him my all. As I spent quiet time with Him one day, He put these words into my heart:

Sing to the Lord, all you people.
Sing a new song to His name.
Sing of His majesty and righteousness, of His might and glory and power.
Sing though your hearts be troubled, though trials come your way.
Sing in celebration, sing in joy, sing in despair, sing in hope.
Sing to Him who gave you life and who gives you eternal salvation.
Sing for He deserves your praise.
Sing for He deserves your worship.
Sing thanks, sing praise, sing to His holy name.

At the time, I had no idea how poignant they would become. What I did know was that a truly blessed life was unlikely to be an easy life. I knew that trials were likely. What's more, I knew that God worked through trials as much as, if not more than, through triumphs. Had the authorities in Jerusalem not tried to stop the followers of Jesus spreading the word, as described in Acts, they would not have been spread further out into the world to influence a wider sphere. Trials can lead to influence and displays of God's sovereignty that are just not available from the standpoint of an easy life.

I wanted to be the person God wanted me to be. I also knew it was highly likely that would not put me on an easy path, but I called on God to help me never underestimate the power and value of each and every difficult day I would face in my life, to never be blinded to the opportunities they brought to grow me, and to never resent the challenges of life. "I know," I prayed, "that trials are far more powerful vehicles for spiritual growth and coming to know You better than easy days are." I longed for God to be always the centre of my world, for nothing to distract me from putting Him first in every aspect of my existence, and that I would forever desire relationship with Him over and above anything else I could want for. I knew, as 2 Corinthians 12:9 told me, "My grace is sufficient for you, for my power is made perfect in weakness." Alone I was weak, yet cleaved to God I felt my strength growing daily.

NINE

Failing to meet society's model

When you're a married woman in your 30s and you're childless it's easy to begin to feel the weight of society's judgement. It seems irrational when you consider that your reproductive system is nobody's business by yours, your husband's and the select people with whom you might choose to share information about it. And yet you can sense the questions in people's minds as they wonder why you haven't got your act together and started a family yet. And there are times when well-meaning people, for reasons I won't even attempt to second guess, go right ahead and voice their questions or opinions aloud. "Isn't it about time you were having babies?" "You ought to get a move on, you know. I know someone who thought they could put off having children and they ended up having to have IVF."

There seems to be an expectation from society that women should seek and achieve motherhood (strangely an expectation that doesn't seem to be transferred to men and fatherhood) and there appears to be an unwritten rule that you're failing in your duty to your fellow humans if you don't achieve it – that, in some way, you are incomplete in your womanhood.

I lost count of the number of times I had to bite my tongue and either smile sweetly or pretend I hadn't heard people's comments or questions. Sometimes, when I was in a less amenable frame of mind, it was a terse "thanks for that." or just a stare that aimed to convey, without saying it outright, a combination of "And this is your business how, exactly?" and "How about we just end this conversation before it's begun?" I don't know exactly how I resisted the urge to give them a very honest, and perhaps very angry, answer, and I know there were plenty of times when all I wanted to do was come back at them with, "Would you like to be the one to let God know He's got His plan for my life wrong? It's just I don't really feel it's my place." And yet, either by the grace of our great God (who, incidentally, has never got a plan, or anything else, wrong) stopping me short of doing something that would put them on the very spot where they'd just dumped me, or as a result of my heart not wanting to be made that publicly vulnerable, I kept my reasons to myself. And, ultimately, that was where they belonged because my childlessness was my business, not that of the questioners.

If I could make one plea through the pages of this book it would be this: Women (and in my experience I can only recall it ever coming from women), please stop pressuring other women about having children and making them feel they're failing you, society or themselves by not doing so. Nobody owes society a child, not

30

everybody wants a child and, perhaps most importantly, nobody has the ultimate say in whether and when they have children. Sure, you can write life goals that say you'd like to marry by 25 and have three children by 30 and you can put your all into trying to achieve those goals, but when push comes to shove you don't hold the key to making them a reality. Babies are not a commodity you can choose off the shelves of a department store or order online to be delivered by a courier. If you have been able to fall pregnant quickly and easily and see that pregnancy through to fruition, it's worth remembering that your story is not typical of every woman. And whether the world needs a mini you, a mini me or a mini anybody else is down to God's design, not ours.

Society's ideals are not God's ideals. Only one set of ideals is perfect and thankfully, when you bear in mind the mess the world is in, it's not society's. And the Bible is a mine of examples where God has challenged society's idea of how things should work and come in with a solution from left field that mankind, from its limited perspective, would think bizarre or even impossible. And, for anyone battling disappointment month in and month out as they seek elusive parenthood, they can be a source of hope and a valuable reminder that, through God, everything is possible.

When God promised Abraham, in Genesis, that he would father a whole nation by his wife Sarah, she was already well past the age at which society would have expected her to become a mother. It's hardly surprising that she did not take the news seriously at first. And yet God knew what He was doing, He knew His plan was perfect and He knew it would come to fruition, just as it did. There's no denying God made Sarah wait a long time to be blessed with a child. Patience, for her, truly was a virtue. And in 1 Samuel we see how God responded when Hannah poured out her heart to Him in prayer for a child. He not only heard her but He granted her the desire of her heart.

I'm not saying that the happy endings in these stories mean that God will give every woman who wants a child the happy ending she desires. I'm not naïve to the fact that some women never fulfil their dream of motherhood. What I am saying is threefold: God can do that which seems impossible, God has a plan for each of our lives which, in its own way, whether we understand it or not, is perfect, and He will make the seemingly-impossible a reality in a person's life if doing so is part of His plan. The key is to trust in Him whatever our circumstances and whatever our longings and be attentive to what He chooses to share of His plans. That knowledge and that trust have given me great hope and strength throughout my journey. Life felt like a rollercoaster, but it was a rollercoaster filled with faith that, at His appointed time, God would come through on the promise we were certain He had made to us and grant us a child.

TEN

Refocusing on God's plan

The words of 1 Thessalonians 5:16-18 instruct us to: "Rejoice always, pray continually, give thanks in all circumstances; for this is God's will for you in Christ Jesus." These words spoke to me in the spring of 2017 as I sought to return my focus to God's plans for the here and now, not being caught up with a single-minded focus in having a child. There was a whole world out there that God wanted me to play my part in and a whole mine of life experience out there to be had if I would just open my heart to opportunities beyond my narrow-minded desire for a child. God had a whole world of adventure lined up for me, if only I would climb on board the train and leave the station. With God at the centre, I knew my life would be perfect. It may not always *seem* perfect but it would *be* perfect.

In my journal God prompted me to write the following words:

God is my strength and my refuge, my help in times of trouble, my precious cornerstone and firm foundation.

I will fear nothing in Him. I rest on His promises daily.
I know His plans for me are perfect.
He will never let me go, leave me or forsake me. He is never-ending.
Though my body may be weak, my heart aching and my mind confused,
He is constant, He is unchanging, He is never shaken.
He will never be shaken.
Trials may come. Hardships may come. My plans may fail but His plans
are always perfect.
In Him I am made perfect to be used for His perfect plans.

I sought to readjust my focus and press in to see what it was that God wanted me to do with my life. I didn't want to be so hung up on my earthly dream of parenthood that I missed God's call on my life for a heavenly purpose. Nor did I want to stop pursuing something I thought wasn't part of His plan for my life if it would turn out that it ultimately was. I sought His clarity on what He wanted me to be and do.

On our fourth wedding anniversary I came across these words, written by Ann Kiemel: "Real success is willingness to accept God's place for us today." They rang so true to me. When we had begun our married life we had undoubtedly expected that we would have at least one child, if not more, after four years. Here we were, four years on, still childless, still longing to know whether we would ever be parents. That which had previously seemed to natural and logical to us had not come to pass.

I called on God to help me accept that parenthood may not be part of His plan for our lives and to be open and attentive to, and eagerly willing to accept, the places and the plan He had set out for us. I wanted to be ready to take on whatever adventure He had lined up for us. I wanted to serve Him joyfully in whatever He had lined up for me. Equally I felt in need of guidance about what that was and where I should be focusing my energy and attention to avoid building up a massive to-do list in seeking to please God and running the risk of turning my life into one like Martha's, I didn't want to lose focus on spending time with God because I was so busy trying to serve Him.

Like so many things, it was easier said than done. I still longed to be a mother. I had no clear sense of whether God wanted that for me or whether He had other plans, although we still clung to the promise we believed He had made. Every time I thought I'd got something clear in my mind something else would come up and throw a spanner in the works of my understanding. I felt like God was giving me the silent treatment. Whether He was speaking to me or not, I certainly wasn't hearing Him. I was desperate to understand, at least to have clarity on something.

In June 2017 I found myself back at the annual women's conference. That weekend, God reminded me clearly that He was in control, He was behind each change of direction my life took – and each time I longed to change direction but couldn't – and His plan was perfect. For the first time in my life God put a song on my heart. As much as I love music, I'd never been able to come up with either song lyrics or melodies before. It simply wasn't my skill. And for that reason alone it was abundantly clear to me that the words I scribbled down in my notebook, ready to transfer to my journal later, and the tune I sang repeatedly in my head for hours until I could get back to my hotel and sing it into the recording app on my phone so I didn't lose the notes, could only have come from God.

Father in Your glory
You're the Author of my story
Lord, have Your way and pour Your love on me

Chorus
You are at work in me, Lord
I feel Your love and see Your glory shine
Draw me closer and if I start to wander
Lord, lead me back into Your loving arms
Your ever-loving arms

Father in Your victory
You orchestrate my symphony
Open my eyes to know Your goodness now

Lord through all my strife
You paint a picture of my life
Draw me to You and never let me go

Lord, let Your glory shine
All through our lives, all over this town
Lord, let Your glory shine
For You are worthy to be known in this place

I didn't know then what God wanted me to do with that song, but I knew I had to keep it safe because eventually He would show me that He wanted me to do something with it. More than that, I knew God was telling me He was in control, He wasn't ignoring me and He was alongside me every step of my journey through life. And I knew it was time for Gary and I to bite a bullet we'd been avoiding for too long.

ELEVEN

Seeking medical answers

For some time Gary and I had pondered whether we should seek medical answers to explain why we had not conceived. It was a dilemma for us. We knew that ultimately it was not doctors, but God who was in control and we knew that, whatever medical assessments revealed, God would decide whether we had a child or not. We didn't relish the idea of facing the questions and tests that seeking medical help would involve. Equally, it raised the question of how far we felt it right for us to pursue parenthood on a medical route and that was a question we were not keen to have to consider, let alone come to a conclusion on.

In summer 2017, though, we knew we needed to bite the bullet. Our longing for a child showed no signs of going away, however much we might try to supress it and focus solely on God. Furthermore, God had not demonstrated to us a clear path for our lives which showed that parenthood was not part of His plan for our future and we were mindful that our last direct communication from Him on the subject had been His leading for us to buy baby clothes and await the child to dress in them.

We took the first steps. Gary attended a GP appointment then went for initial tests to provide details that would be needed when we visited a gynaecologist. I attended a GP appointment and was referred for that gynaecology appointment. The waiting time for an appointment was not short. We received our referral confirmation from the GPs surgery in August with instruction to contact the hospital if nobody had been in touch by mid-September. The wait for an appointment, we would learn, was around 12 weeks. Twelve weeks. Three more potentially-lost opportunities before we began in earnest the journey of understanding – or at least trying to understand – the reasons for our lack of conception.

I tried to be positive about things but still I couldn't help thinking that time was being wasted. Perhaps we should have started trying for a baby sooner. Perhaps we should have sought help sooner. But, at the same time, I knew everything was in God's hands and His timing was perfect. It was just easier said than done remembering that perfection and immediacy were not the same thing.

Eventually we received an appointment date: November 14, 2017. Later this was rescheduled to November 17, 2017. All we could do was wait, hope and pray.

TWELVE

Waiting on God

As we took the initial steps on the path to medical answers, we felt a bit more relaxed in our quest for parenthood. We knew there could still be a long road ahead of us, and not necessarily an easy one, but it was no longer entirely in our hands to try to make things happen.

As we waited for the appointments we needed before we could visit the gynaecologist, I spent a lot of time waiting on God and seeking His guidance for the road ahead. And, after so many months of confusion and what seemed like silence from Him, I began to hear from Him so clearly.

In those weeks I spent a lot of time with God at my favourite lakeside beauty spot – reading and studying His Word, praying and waiting on Him. And among other things He put on my heart two songs, the words of which, though poignant then on the path we were still walking, would take on a far greater significance in the months to come.

From Mountain Top to Valley Deep

From mountain top to valley deep
When the going is light and when the path is steep
Throughout my toil and in my sleep
Faithfully beside me You remain
Faithfully beside me You remain

Chorus
You are never changing God
You are faithfulness forever
And when I live my toughest days
You always carry me

When I ride Your waves and when the swell drags me
With my feet on solid ground or when I feel all at sea
When I stand up tall or when I fall on bended knee
Every step Your victory I claim
Every step Your victory I claim

When my days are bright and when the darkness comes
Even when the shadow of my earthly death looms
Hung upon Your cross and risen from Your tomb
You have gone before to break my chains
You have gone before to break my chains

Still Waters

You are the still waters of my life
When all around me changes, Lord
When turmoil comes

Your sustaining love and grace remain

Chorus
You never fail me, Lord
You never let me go
Even on the darkest path
You daily walk beside

You are the firm anchor of my hope
When storms are raging all around
When winds of torment blow
Your firm-holding mooring lines hold strong

You are the deep peace within my heart
When I begin to doubt myself
When questions fill my mind
You draw near to fill me with Your love

You are the bright light that shows my way
When darkness tries to cover me
When I cannot find my path
You lift the clouds that try to block the sun

We knew God was in control and we waited, joyfully, patiently and faithfully, on God and for the answers we so desperately desired.

THIRTEEN

The happiest day

On October 4, 2017 things changed. As with every month, I'd been keeping a close eye on the calendar and keeping alert for signs of whether we were about to face our now-regular round of disappointment. This month something was different. The symptoms that usually spelled the imminent arrival of discontent and frustration were different, somehow. I didn't want to jump in too early with assumptions – I'd done that before and reality hit hard when I was wrong – but as each day passed I grew more and more hopeful.

Then, when I felt I'd let sufficient days pass to be fairly certain about what it was going to tell me, I decided to do a pregnancy test to find out for certain. I would do it that night. I texted Gary from the office and told him I'd pick up dinner on my way home. I carried on with my work, counting down the hours and minutes until I could find out for certain that about which I was already pretty sure.

I left work and headed for the next town. The network of people we knew meant it would be virtually impossible to buy a pregnancy test in our hometown without risking bumping into one of them and I didn't want anyone knowing our news until we were ready to tell them. I went to a supermarket, bought a test, went home and dashed straight to the bathroom to use it.

After what seemed like the longest three minutes of my life I stood, positive pregnancy test in hand, stupid grin on face, trying to get my head around what the little white stick was telling me: there was a tiny human growing inside me, finally, and I was going to be a mum. And, for good measure, I did the second test in the pack, partly to be sure, partly to confirm my estimate of dates was correct.

I ran to the bedroom to grab something I had prepared months earlier for this occasion. Test sticks safely inside with the other contents of the pregnancy-announcement gift box, I ran downstairs and presented it to Gary. For some reason I thought it would be a surprise. Apparently I'd forgotten that my husband can A) read calendars, B) count, C) realise that I'm up to something when I dash straight upstairs having barely said hello, and D) tell when I'm trying and failing to hide a massive grin of delight. He thought he knew what I was presenting him with. He was right. We were both overjoyed. Maybe a bit terrified but overjoyed nonetheless.

After a few minutes, we knew we had to get back to the reality of day-to-day life. Gary had a night shift to get to. We had to eat.

"We'd better have dinner," I said. "What are we having?" Gary asked. Ah, I thought, I knew there was something else I was meant to get at the supermarket. Baby brain had arrived with a vengeance. A mad dash to another supermarket was in order to pick up a now-celebratory pizza.

"Thank you" seemed nowhere near sufficient as we thanked God for the answer to prayer He had given us in the little miracle growing in my womb. We knew it was still early days but we felt sure He was going to protect our little one and we prayed for His help as we did our best to keep our little child safe.

Four days later we were able to share our news with our prayer partners – the only people we planned to tell until after our 12-week scan. The announcement had been so long coming and at the same time it felt so surreal that we were able to make it.

FOURTEEN

Eager anticipation

The following weeks were a blur of excitement as we set out to get our heads around our seemingly-changing circumstances. There were countless online searches for information: what to eat and what to avoid eating, the developmental stages of pregnancy, the practicalities of maternity leave and pay and so much more. There was so much to get our heads around. We would need to buy a car, but what car? We would need to decorate a nursery, buy furniture, a pram, everything a baby would need. We started to rein in our day-to-day spending, conscious that our income was set to nosedive, at least temporarily.

We were so thankful for our answer to prayer and so happy. We prayed that God would keep our tiny baby safe and look after us all in the weeks and months ahead. We were careful not to get carried away, knowing the risks and statistics that surrounded miscarriage, yet we couldn't resist buying the odd bargain baby outfit we came across in the shops and online.

And we had faith that we would need them. After all, God had led us to buy that first little outfit and we'd taken that as a promise that we would one day be able to put it to use.

Appointments were made with the doctor and midwife. I stopped doing things I would normally have done – lifting and carrying, moving furniture, working long hours and staying up late. Although nobody said anything I became certain that everyone around me had twigged that I was pregnant. But they hadn't and our happy news remained the knowledge of just me and Gary, two trusted friends and the medical professionals involved.

At six weeks we began to refer to our baby as Lentil. Half nickname, half code word that could be used with our trusted friends, it reflected the little one's size at the time. The embryo may have grown week on week but the name stuck.

On November 1, just over eight weeks into the pregnancy, I had my first midwife appointment. It was an exciting but nerve-wracking day. We discussed how the next 32 weeks or so should pan out – the appointments that should be to come, the scans, where we would like our baby to be born... Suddenly everything became so real and so immense. We were going to be parents. It was a position we'd always hoped to find ourselves in but one we still couldn't believe was happening. And yet it was and we needed to prepare.

I had paperwork coming out of my ears: A booklet to take to all appointments that would track every detail of my pregnancy, all manner of information leaflets, coupons to sign up to various retailers' loyalty schemes for new parents, and the one thing everyone hopes they will never need – the phone number to use in a pregnancy-related emergency.

A date was set for our first scan – Friday, December 1, 12-and-a-half weeks into the pregnancy. We faced a month-long wait to see our tiny baby for the first time. We were excited about what lay ahead.

Little did we know, as I sat in that first midwife appointment, that our tiny baby had probably already died.

FIFTEEN

The hardest day

November 16, 2017 was a day that began like any other. A busy day at work beckoned. I woke with my alarm and got out of bed. I was 10-and-a-half weeks pregnant, just 15 days away from my first scan and excited for the future. But as I got ready for the day ahead I was to discover the first hint of that which would soon stop me in my tracks. The tiniest show of blood set into motion a chain of events that would take me, over the course of about 28 hours, from joyful expectation to deepest despair.

At first I thought nothing of it. I knew I should get it checked out, for peace of mind, but I never suspected anything would be wrong. It was so tiny and I was so sure God had been telling me He would keep this baby safe.

I made an urgent appointment for a short time later and rang my boss to warn her I'd be late in because of it. She asked if I was okay. My simple reply, "I hope so," gave no indication of the enormity of what was to come. Quite simply, I had no idea of the enormity of what was to come.

At my appointment I was referred to the nearby early pregnancy assessment clinic for a precautionary scan the following day. I still had no expectation that things would be anything other than okay. I felt no different.

I went on to work. It was a Thursday like any other. I didn't dwell particularly on the following day's appointment. That evening we realised that the appointment clashed with something my husband was meant to be doing for church. We didn't want him to not be able to attend. We were expecting this to be the first time we saw our tiny baby and we wanted to share that experience. We knew there was a chance we might receive bad news – albeit one we weren't expecting to happen – and we knew that if that was the case we needed to be together. A couple of quick phone calls later, someone was lined up to stand in for him. That person was oblivious to the detail of why Gary needed him to stand in. We were oblivious to just how important it would be that Gary was at my side the next day.

We woke the next day still feeling positive. I headed for work as normal and, when the time came, Gary met me outside the office and we headed to the hospital together. We were happy. We sat in the waiting room smiling and laughing about things. Maybe it was a subconscious defence mechanism kicking in to keep us upbeat right up to the point when the rug would be pulled out from under us and we would come crashing to the ground feeling like we'd never be happy again. Maybe we were just refusing to face up to the potential reality that lay before us.

Despite the waiting room being virtually empty, we had a little wait. It was ironic, we noted, given that a sign on the wall stated that the average waiting time was zero minutes and the action for the week ahead was to reduce waiting times. Eventually we were called through.

As I underwent the initial scan Gary could see the tiny baby on the screen. We were reassured. He was there (our little one had always been "he" in my mind). That must be a good thing, right? We never imagined it wouldn't be. A second scan was carried out to get a closer view. As the consultant gathered the information he needed, we thought maybe he would tell us that there was something wrong with our baby, that perhaps he'd have some condition or other. We never imagined, knowing he was there, the news that was to come.

And then it came. Bad news. A miscarriage. I should have been 10 and a half weeks pregnant but we were told our baby had stopped growing at eight weeks. We'd always assumed that if you miscarried a baby it wouldn't be there anymore. We'd never thought about there being a process involved and that process taking time. Now we knew how wrong we'd been.

The rest of the day was an emotional rollercoaster. There were practical things to deal with – discussing the options for the next steps with medical staff, contacting my bosses who were expecting me back at the office, remembering to eat (never has a trip to the chip shop been so devoid of any positive feeling), searching the house for tissues and wondering why we didn't keep a bigger stock in reserve for this type of occasion. Mostly, though, it was a day of contemplation, of crying more tears than we thought our eyes could ever produce, of clinging to each other as we'd never done before, and of leaning on God.

As everything we had hoped for appeared to be being wrenched from our grasp and we struggled to understand why, we turned, from the outset, to God. We could have turned our backs on Him at that moment, questioned why He would put us through such heartache and sought to blame Him, but we knew we couldn't do that. We knew that God's love was there to carry us through difficult circumstances, not prevent us from experiencing them, and we had every faith that He would do that. Proverbs 3:5-6 says: "Trust in the Lord with all your heart and lean not on your own understanding; in all your ways acknowledge him and he will make straight your paths." Sometimes it's not easy to see through circumstances but in everything, good and bad, I knew He loved me and had my best interests at heart. He alone was my heart's primary desire, far beyond a child or anything else I might like to have. We knew, as Romans 8:28 told us: "that in all things God works for the good of those who love him, who have been called according to his purpose."

SIXTEEN

The week that followed

The days immediately after our first visit to the hospital were filled with challenges and competing emotions. We didn't pretend to understand what was happening to us or to know exactly why. The fact that our baby was still in my womb left two possible outcomes to our situation: the miscarriage could complete in time, either naturally or with assistance, or God could come through with a miracle and renew that child's life. Whichever it was to be, we were certain God would work through it to bring about good in one way or another. We just needed to be patient and have faith that that would be the case.

There were things we needed to do in those days: arrange time off work, share the news with our immediate family, meet up with our ever-faithful prayer partners and bring them up to speed with events. Most of all, though, we needed to rest, both physically and on God, and those days brought some of the most wonderful, albeit at times unfathomable, times with Him that I had ever experienced. It might have been one of the hardest times of our lives, but it was also a period when we were blessed with the time and space to focus first and foremost on the Lord for much of every day. And that, whatever the circumstances, is a blessed position to be in.

Sleep wasn't always easy to come by in those early days. Often I found myself getting to sleep with relative ease, exhausted from a day of heartache and tears, but I also found myself waking most days before sunrise, often around 5.30am, and being unable to get back to sleep. Rising before the sun, when we didn't need to, seemed somehow unnatural, and we were keen to keep as much normality in our daily routine as we could, so we would lie there thinking, praying, talking things over, listening to music or a combination of all four.

Within a couple of days God began to make things clearer in our minds. There came a point where I began to know in my heart that, though I knew God was more than capable of performing a miracle, that wasn't to be His plan in this case. I developed a sense that His plan was to bring good from our circumstances rather than to alter them. I trusted Him, I knew He knew best and I allowed myself to grieve for our baby rather than clinging to a hope that things would return to how they had been. As I processed my thoughts, I wrote them in what would be my one and only letter to my beloved child:

> *My dearest darling Lentil,*
> *I hardly know where to begin. Just a few days ago we were*
> *eagerly awaiting our dating scan on December 1 so we could see*

you for the very first time and begin in earnest the preparations for your arrival. Then on Friday we found ourselves looking at your lifeless form on the scanner screen as we received the worst news imaginable that God had called you home to Him before we'd even had the chance to see or feel you move, let alone hold you in our arms.

We'd talked about giving you that all-important skin-to-skin contact in your first hours to help us bond. We never dreamed we'd be left with only a tiny, grainy picture to remember our precious baby by. And yet we will always treasure that picture. That which to anyone else might just show an indistinguishable blur is identifiable to us as our beautiful, precious, much-loved baby, 50% Mummy, 50% Daddy but 100% gifted to us by God.

We always knew God would only ever loan a child to us to care for on His behalf, but how we longed to have you a season longer. We longed to watch you grow and to be the ones to introduce you to the love of God, encouraging you to explore His Word and press in to experience that love for yourself and come to the point of salvation from sin. Now we see it was God's plan to call you straight home to Him by grace, without you even needing to set foot on this fallen planet.

Darling child, we wanted Earth to have a Lentil but He knew it was Heaven, not Earth, that needed you.

There are so many things we may never know – whether you'd have been a boy or a girl (I always thought boy but Daddy would say girl), what colour your eyes and hair would have been, how many sleepless nights you'd have caused us over the years – but amid all the lack of knowing we know one thing for certain, that our loss is Heaven's gain, and your gain because there is no better place to be.

God's perfect plan was that you would never have a true home in our house but you will always, without a shadow of a doubt, have a place in our hearts. God may grant us more children, we just don't know, but you, Lentil, will always be our baby number one, not simply pregnancy number one.

In the short time you were with us you made me feel so alive, so happy, so excited for the future and I will be eternally grateful, both to God and to you, for that. I don't know how long it will be before I can feel that way again, but I count it a great comfort in these difficult days to know that you are safe in the arms of the loving Father who will never leave you or forsake you. You are in the place I always hoped you would end up in, you just got there by a quicker, easier route than I ever imagined.

I'm sorry, my darling child, that we never got as far as choosing you a real name – Lentil was only meant to be a pet name until we could look into your eyes and settle on what to call you – but now you will be known by the precious name God had chosen for you before he even placed you in my womb. That womb feels so empty now but I know Heaven must feel even more alive.

Whatever your Heavenly name, you will always be our little Lentil and I promise you I will carry your memory in my heart always.

I like to think you might be watching over us and seeing how much you are loved by us but even if you don't know our love, I know that you know the love of He who loves you so much more and so much better than we ever could.

We will never understand in this life why you were taken from us, but I feel honoured and privileged to be able to call myself your mum in this life and I know it will all become clear when I reach the next.

Until we meet again, precious one...

All my love, Mummy

xXx

As time moved on, we knew we needed to as well. We had left the hospital the previous Thursday intending to let nature take its course and return two weeks later to ensure that had happened. Three days in, with no sign of progress, we decided to move forward our follow-up appointment and take steps to end the sense of limbo we were in. We knew we couldn't fully move forward all the time we were still physically holding on to this pregnancy. We couldn't wholly grieve for the baby we had lost, and we couldn't begin to think about the possibility of another baby, until there was physical progress.

We returned to the hospital on November 23 for a follow-up scan that confirmed there had been no change. We had confirmation of that which, by then, we knew in our hearts; that God wasn't going to come through with a miracle that would see our baby's earthly life restored. Paperwork followed and I was booked in to be admitted the following day to be given medication that would prompt the miscarriage to complete. I had no reservations about the procedure by then. I knew I could not have gone through the procedure the previous week as I would have been left with a lingering "what if?" in my mind; what if there'd been a mistake or what if God wanted us to have faith for a miracle and we didn't allow Him the space? Now we knew for certain there was no chance of our baby surviving on Earth. More than that, we knew that our beloved baby was already safely in the arms of the loving Saviour. Ultimately, our baby was in a better place than we were. He had no need for his earthly body now. We had no need to hold on to it. We began in earnest our preparations for the following day. Lifts were arranged, a bag packed, snacks gathered (on the nurse's advice because, well, hospital food...). We were as ready as we would ever be.

SEVENTEEN

Letting Lentil go

As we returned from hospital that Thursday, we decided it was time to say our goodbyes to Lentil. Losing him so early meant there would be no funeral or formal service to remember him. There would be few memories to be shared, for so few people knew he had even existed. But we knew he had existed and, far beyond that, had brought so much to our lives, and we needed to mark that.

We visited an engraver and chose a padlock which he engraved with the simple words: "To Lentil, love always, Mummy & Daddy xx". We visited a florist a bought a single yellow gerbera – a bright, happy colour for someone who had brought so much sunshine and happiness into our lives, albeit for such a short time. And then we set off to walk to the shore, to put our tribute at a memorial cross on the hill overlooking the water – a place that was already home to many remembrance padlocks.

It was a windy day and as we neared the sea it began to rain. A passer-by remarked that we'd perhaps chosen the wrong day for a walk. We said we'd be fine. I was hit with a single-minded determination to do what I had set out to do, come what may. Right then, I needed to leave this tribute. I needed to make sure Lentil couldn't be forgotten. I needed the sense of closure that this act of both thanksgiving and remembrance would bring. So we continued up the hill, and it began to hail, and the hail hurt, and the rain and hail drenched the florist's paper surrounding the flower, and the wind threatened to snap the flower, and our patience frayed a little, but we made it up the hill. And, with wind and rain whipping at our faces and mixing with the tears streaming down them, we placed our tribute, pledged never to forget our little Lentil, and headed home. We were wet through, we were shivering, but we had done what needed to be done.

Back at home we psyched ourselves up for the following day's hospital visit, but we needn't have bothered. The next morning I woke early, as had become my new custom, and found that things had progressed naturally and we were able to cancel the hospital admission. In just a couple of hours I knew that Lentil's tiny earthly body had passed from mine in the final act of letting him go. I knew God was in that, and I was certain He had been waiting for us to have that sense of closure we had allowed ourselves to reach the day before, to be able to say, "Okay, they're ready now." It was as though Lentil was saying, "It's okay, I see that you're ready to let me go now." And, in a strange way, it was kind of nice. I'm not saying the whole thing wasn't heartbreaking and traumatic, because it was and I hope I never have to go through it again, but, given that we knew it had to happen, the way in which it happened was just perfect in timing, location and everything else. There's a lot to be said for being able to spend the day in the comfort of your own house instead of spending the day in a sterile hospital being dosed up on drugs and feeling devoid of dignity.

Over the days that followed we focused on sharing our news more widely, first with our church family, then colleagues, then our wider friends, and I returned to work in the pursuit of some sense of normality as we came to terms with everything we had faced and everything we were still to face. We knew it would be a difficult journey, but even in the sadness we saw God working through the situation in the ways He allowed others to be impacted by our testimony of His love through our circumstances, and in the way He led others to share their similar testimonies with us. We still had a long way to go in grieving for Lentil, and in renewing our pursuit of parenthood, but already we could see good coming from our loss.

EIGHTEEN

Reflections on a blessed journey

In the weeks after losing Lentil I learned something new about the way God works in people's lives. It's quite possible that I should have realised this long ago and I was just slow on the uptake, but in these circumstances I saw it clearer than I could ever have seen it before. I used to look around, at church and in other areas of life, and see people who, by and large, I could learn from. Most had more life experience than me. I never saw the reverse; that others could learn from me. I never saw myself as having anything to offer on that level, being so devoid, in relative terms, of life experience, and I definitely never saw it as a mutual relationship of learning from one another.

But, after losing Lentil and reading and hearing the responses to our news that we had from people within our church family, as well as outside it, I realised that I'd been blessed with life experience that not everyone had had, and with that came the opportunity for all sorts of people – young, old, Christian or not –

to be blessed by my experience. And in that moment I knew I had a responsibility to be real and not keep my experiences under my hat because somewhere, somehow, someone could be blessed by that. I might never fully know who or how and that didn't matter.

On November 26, a question came into my mind: If I could turn back time, erase the events of the past couple of weeks and put myself on a path to the outcome we always wanted for our pregnancy, would I do it? In all honesty, I knew the answer was no – for two reasons. Number one, that was our plan, that wasn't God's plan, and I knew my plans would never measure up to His. Number two, I had learned and been blessed by so much in the previous 12 days that I wouldn't have benefited from if things had gone to our plan. It had been a costly and painful learning curve, but I would not have been without it for anything.

Two days later, I revisited my not-even-Christmas list from September 2016. I looked at the top prayer request – to be blessed with a baby – and without much pondering I crossed it off because I knew God had granted that prayer in the shape of our precious Lentil. He might not have done it in quite the way we had anticipated or hoped, but there was no questioning that He'd done it and our lives had been forever changed and forever blessed by our darling baby's existence. That didn't mean we didn't still want a child to bring up, though, so at the bottom of my not-even-Christmas list I added a new prayer – to be blessed with a baby of our own who would be brought to birth for us to raise on Earth. Yes, we had learned a valuable lesson about being specific in our prayers.

God had given us Lentil and God had taken him away. We knew He would only ever loan a child to us to care for for a season. We had longed for it to be a longer season but God knew best and we knew His plan was perfect. We knew something else, as well. Sometimes there are points in our lives when we need to have something we value taken from our grasp to focus our minds on the abundant blessings that we have. We were, and we remain, truly blessed.

Looking back over my journals at the journey God had brought us on, in the weeks after our miscarriage I came across the songs He had put on my heart over the summer. Suddenly the words of From Mountain Top to Valley Deep and Still Waters took on a whole new complexion. Through the words of those songs I sensed God speaking directly into my heart and saying, "See, I told you I'd be there, you know I have been and you know I will be." And I knew it was true.

NINETEEN

God confirms His faithfulness

In the days that followed our miscarriage I looked for evidence of that which I thought I was right in understanding: that our precious child was with God. I knew that I knew it, but I still needed to check it against the evidence. If someone questioned how I knew, I needed a better response than, "I just know".

Among the evidence I found was Psalm 145:9, "The Lord is good to all; he has compassion on all he has made." I knew that a god who is good and compassionate to all could not possibly set any other path for a child who never needed nor had the opportunity to repent of earthly sin than to take him home to Him.

And, as an added bonus at a time when I felt like my world was falling apart around me, the rest of the psalm contained plenty of reminders about God's greatness and how worthy He is of our praise whatever our circumstances. It was welcome confirmation that I was on the right track.

Before this, in October 2017, Lou Fellingham performed a concert at my in-laws' church in Dorset and for Christmas they gave me a CD they'd bought there. Inside the CD case, when I opened it, was a flier for the concert, with a note written on it to me by Lou, including the phrase "Psalm 145", the psalm on which one of the songs on the CD was based. I thought nothing of it at Christmas.

It wasn't until mid-January 2018 that I made any connection. Looking at the note again I was prompted to read Psalm 145 and I realised it was the passage I had gone to in November. But, as I read on, it seemed strangely familiar, like I'd been reading more recently than that.

When I checked back in my journal, I found it written out in full twice; once on November 22, just five days after we learned of our miscarriage, and once on New Year's Day, sitting on the page that faces a song for Lentil, written just the day before.

In that moment I sensed God saying, "I know you already know but, just in case you're ever not sure, see, I had this in hand long before you ever knew you were going to face it."

That concert, the day that note was written, was three days after we found out I was pregnant.

I knew He had been at my side every step of the way, but now I had evidence that surpassed my indwelt knowledge and provided a tangible reminder if my knowledge and faith ever wavered. God knows what we need long before we ever do.

"The Lord is near to all who call on him, to all who call on him in truth." Psalm 145:18

Epilogue

Gary's thoughts

The weeks following Lentil's loss were a time of life spent refocusing and moving back towards how things were before both the joy of our pregnancy and sadness of its end. It was a time of togetherness for us both, reflecting on our loss and looking to the future with many tears and prayers.

We have found comfort in God's Word, including Matthew 5:4 which tells us, "Blessed are those who mourn, for they will be comforted."

There have been times of despair, where no path seemed like the right one to take, and others where He made the path so clear.

We do not know exactly what God's plans are for us when it comes to parenthood but trust in Him for that and, in the words of 2 Corinthians 5:7, "live by faith, not by sight". As our lives move forward we remain faithful in our prayers for new life to come when He is ready.

Our experiences brought with them pain and heartache that were inevitable in such circumstances and left us with some questions we cannot yet answer, but we remain safe and secure in the knowledge of Romans 8:18: "I consider that our present sufferings are not worth comparing with the glory that will be revealed in us."